® Landoll, Inc.
Ashland, Ohio 44805
© 1995 Coombe Books Ltd.

AMERICA'S BEST

Healthy

E A T I N G

Introduction

With magazines and newspapers regularly publishing articles expounding the latest theories about what foods we should or should not eat and why, there can be said to be no lack of information on what is believed to constitute a healthy diet. Yet, sadly, much of the advice with which we are bombarded is contradictory, leaving many puzzled as to what they should be eating to enjoy the best of health.

Variety is at the heart of a pattern of healthy eating. As no one type of food contains all the proteins, fats, carbohydrates, vitamins, and minerals needed by the body, it is vital to eat a wide variety of foodstuffs to ensure that the balance needed to keep the body healthy is maintained.

Protein is essential for the well-being of the body, promoting the growth and repair of tissues and, among other things, helping to make the antibodies which enable the body to fight infection. Meat, fish, and dairy products are all good sources of protein, and ones with which most people are familiar. Grains, pulses, and nuts, however, also contain some proteins (though they are not complete proteins and must be eaten in the correct combinations in order for the body to get maximum benefit.) Modern diets tend to rely too heavily on animal proteins and neglect vegetable proteins, which contain no cholesterol or saturated fat. A healthy diet should use vegetable proteins to make up a larger proportion of the body's protein requirement and reduce the intake of fat-rich, animal proteins.

It is also important to try to reduce the amount of red meat included in your diet, as it contains high levels of saturated fat and cholesterol. Cholesterol, a fat-like substance, is transported around the body in the bloodstream. Though small amounts of cholesterol are necessary for the correct functioning of the body, a high level in the blood stream may lead to cholesterol deposits in the blood vessels. A build-up of such fatty deposits thickens the walls of the vessels, making it harder for the heart to pump blood around the body and so putting it under strain. Although no conclusive link between dietary cholesterol and levels of cholesterol in the blood has been established, it is wise to substitute meats which are known to be low in cholesterol, such as chicken, or to eat fish, particularly fatty fish such as mackerel, containing oils which are believed to be cholesterol reducing.

Fresh fruit and vegetables play an important role in a well-balanced diet and there is much truth in the adage "An apple a day keeps the doctor away." Both fruits and vegetables are a good source of fiber and are rich in the vitamins and minerals needed for the body to function properly.

A good, well-balanced diet is the key to a long and healthy life and, as the wide range of delicious recipes in this book shows, food that is healthy need never be tasteless or lacking in imagination. The selection of starters, meat and fish dishes, as well as desserts, in this book provides the perfect introduction to the delights of healthy eating.

Gazpacho

SERVES 4

Gazpacho is a typically Spanish soup which is served well chilled, accompanied by a selection of fresh vegetables.

PREPARATION: 20 mins, plus chilling

1 pound ripe tomatoes
1 onion, chopped
1 green pepper, diced
½ cucumber, chopped
2 tbsps day-old white breadcrumbs
2 cloves garlic, crushed
2 tbsps red wine vinegar
2½ cups tomato juice
Salt and freshly ground black pepper

Accompaniments
½ cucumber, diced
10 green onions (scallions), chopped
2 cups tomatoes, skinned, seeded and chopped
1 large green bell pepper, diced

1. Cut a small cross in the top of each of the tomatoes, and plunge into a bowl of boiling water for a few seconds.

2. Carefully peel the skin away from the blanched tomatoes. Discard the skin and chop the tomatoes coarsely, removing the tough cores.

Step 2
Carefully peel the skin away from the blanched tomatoes using a sharp knife.

3. Put the roughly-chopped tomatoes into a liquidizer or food processor, along with the onion, pepper, and cucumber. Blend until finely chopped.

4. Put the chopped vegetables into a bowl with the breadcrumbs, garlic, vinegar, and tomato juice. Mix well to blend evenly and allow to stand 15 minutes.

5. Season the soup thoroughly, then push through a fine-meshed sieve, using the back of a wooden spoon and working well to press all the vegetables through, but keeping the seeds out of the resulting purée.

6. Chill the soup well before serving, surrounded by bowls containing the accompaniments.

Mediterranean Eggplant

SERVES 2-4

These delicious stuffed eggplants can be served as an accompaniment to a main meal for four or as a lunch dish for two.

PREPARATION: 25 mins
COOKING: 40 mins

2 small eggplants
2 tbsps polyunsaturated margarine
1 small onion, finely chopped
1 clove garlic, crushed
2 tomatoes, skinned
⅔ cup long-grain rice, cooked
2 tsps fresh marjoram, chopped
Pinch of cinnamon
Salt and freshly ground black pepper

1. Wrap the eggplants in foil and bake in an oven preheated to 350°F for 20 minutes or until softened. Allow to cool.

2. Cut the eggplants in half lengthwise then using a serrated teaspoon or grapefruit knife, carefully scoop out the pulp leaving a ½-inch border to form a shell.

3. Melt the margarine in a skillet and gently sauté the onion and garlic until they are just soft.

4. Chop the eggplant pulp roughly and stir into the skillet along with the onions. Cover and cook about 5 minutes.

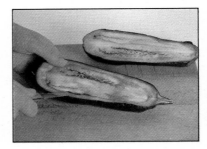

Step 2
Carefully scoop the pulp out of each eggplant half with a serrated spoon or grapefruit knife.

5. Quarter the tomatoes and remove and discard the seeds. Chop the tomato flesh roughly and stir into the cooked eggplant and onion mixture, along with the cooked rice, marjoram, and cinnamon. Season with salt and pepper.

6. Carefully pile the rice filling into the eggplant shells and arrange them in an ovenproof dish or on a baking tray. Cover with foil.

7. Return to the oven and bake 20 minutes. Serve hot, garnished with a little finely chopped parsley if wished.

Tomato and Pepper Ice

SERVES 4-6

Similar to frozen gazpacho, this appetizer is ideal for serving on warm summer days.

PREPARATION: 15 mins plus 2 hrs freezing

---

6 ice cubes
½ cup canned tomato juice
Juice of 1 lemon
1 tsp Worcestershire sauce
½ small green pepper, very finely chopped
½ small red pepper, very finely chopped

---

1. Put the ice into a thick plastic bag and break into small pieces using a rolling pin or steak hammer.

2. Put the broken ice into a blender or food processor, along with the tomato juice, lemon juice, and Worcestershire sauce. Blend the mixture until it becomes slushy.

Step 2 Blend the ice, tomato juice, lemon juice, and Worcestershire sauce until it becomes a smooth slush.

Step 5 During the freezing time, keep stirring the tomato and pepper ice with a fork.

3. Pour the tomato mixture into ice trays and freeze 30 minutes, or until it is just half-frozen.

4. Remove the tomato ice from the freezer trays and put it into a bowl. Mash the tomato ice with the back of a fork until the crystals are well broken up.

5. Mix in the chopped peppers and return the tomato ice to the freezer trays. Re-freeze for a further 1½ hours, stirring occasionally to prevent the mixture from solidifying completely.

6. To serve, allow the tomato ice to defrost about 5 minutes, then mash with the back of a fork to roughly break up the ice crystals. Serve in small chilled glass dishes or in tomato shells.

Zucchini, Caper, and Anchovy Salad

SERVES 4

The secret of this salad is to slice the raw zucchini really thinly.

PREPARATION: 15-20 mins

1 pound zucchini
1 small onion, thinly sliced
1 tbsp capers
4-6 canned anchovy fillets, chopped
1 tbsp anchovy oil (drained from the can of
   anchovy fillets)
2 tbsps olive oil
2 tbsps tarragon vinegar
Juice of ½ lemon
Salt and freshly ground black pepper to taste

1. Top and tail the zucchini, and slice them very thinly with a sharp knife, food processor, or mandolin.

2. Mix the sliced zucchini with the onion, capers and chopped anchovy fillets.

3. Mix the anchovy oil, olive oil, tarragon vinegar, and lemon juice together; add salt and pepper to taste.

4. Stir the dressing into the prepared salad ingredients.

Salade Paysanne

SERVES 6

This salad can be made with any selection of fresh vegetables, so whether it's winter or summer, there's no excuse for not serving a delicious fresh salad.

PREPARATION: 20 mins

4 green onions (scallions)
½ cucumber
3 carrots
6 large tomatoes, skinned
10 button mushrooms
3 sticks celery
1 green pepper, chopped
15-20 tiny cauliflower flowerets
15-20 baby radishes, quartered
1 tbsp chopped watercress, cress, or chia
2 sprigs fresh coriander (cilantro), or parsley, chopped
8 lettuce leaves for garnish

Dressing
½ tsp salt
½ tsp freshly ground black pepper
2 tbsps cider or wine vinegar
1 tbsp lemon juice
4 tbsps olive or vegetable oil
Pinch powdered mustard
Liquid sweetener to taste

1. Trim the green onions and slice them diagonally into thin slices.

2. Peel the cucumber and quarter it lengthwise. Use a sharp knife to remove the

Step 6 Whisk all the dressing ingredients together using a fork or balloon whisk, until the mixture becomes thick and cloudy.

soft, seedy center, discard this, and dice the remaining flesh.

3. Peel the carrots and slice them thinly, cutting the carrots diagonally with a sharp knife.

4. Quarter the skinned tomatoes and cut away the tough green cores.

5. Thinly slice the mushrooms and celery. Cut the pepper in half lengthwise, discard the seeds and stringy parts then chop the flesh.

6. Mix together all the dressing ingredients. Whisk thoroughly using a fork, or balloon whisk, until the mixture becomes thick and cloudy.

7. Arrange the lettuce leaves on a serving dish. Mix all the prepared vegetables together, and pile on top.

8. Just before serving, spoon a little of the dressing over the salad and serve the remainder separately in a small jug.

Vegetable and Olive Casserole

SERVES 6

The addition of vinegar and capers gives this refreshing vegetable dish a sharp twist to its flavor.

PREPARATION: 30 mins plus standing time
COOKING: 25 mins

---

1 eggplant
Salt
⅔ cup olive or sunflower oil
1 onion, thinly sliced
2 red bell peppers, chopped
2 sticks celery, thickly sliced
1 pound canned plum tomatoes, chopped and
   sieved
2 tbsps red wine vinegar
1 tbsp sugar
1 clove garlic, crushed
Salt and freshly ground black pepper
12 pitted black olives, quartered
1 tbsp capers

---

1. Cut the eggplant in half lengthwise and score the cut surface deeply, in a lattice fashion, with the point of a sharp knife.

Step 1 Score the cut surface of the eggplants in a lattice pattern, using the point of a sharp knife.

Step 6 Simmer the casserole, uncovered, over a low heat until the juice has thickened and reduced.

2. Sprinkle the cut surface liberally with salt, and leave to stand 30 minutes. Rinse thoroughly under running water, then pat dry and cut it into 1-inch cubes.

3. Heat the oil in a large skillet and add the onion, peppers, and celery. Cook gently about 5 minutes, stirring occasionally, until the vegetables have softened but not browned.

4. Add the eggplant to the pan and mix well to coat thoroughly with the oil. Continue cooking gently 5 minutes.

5. Add the sieved tomatoes to the pan, along with the remaining ingredients, except for the olives and capers. Cover and simmer 5 minutes.

6. Add the olives and capers and continue cooking gently, uncovered, 15 minutes, or until most of the liquid has evaporated and the sauce has thickened and reduced.

Seviche

SERVES 4

In this traditional Mexican dish, the raw fish is "cooked" in a mixture of oil and lime juice.

PREPARATION: 20 mins plus 24 hrs standing time

1 pound fresh cod or red fillet, skinned
Juice and grated rind of 2 limes
1 small shallot, finely chopped
1 green chili, seeded and finely chopped
1 tsp ground coriander
1 small green pepper, sliced
1 small red pepper, sliced
4 green onions (scallions), finely chopped
1 tbsp chopped parsley
1 tbsp chopped coriander (cilantro)
2 tbsps olive oil
Freshly ground black pepper
1 small lettuce, to serve

1. Using a sharp knife, cut the fish into very thin strips across the grain. Put the strips into a large bowl and pour the lime juice over them.

Step 1 Cut the fish fillet across the grain into very thin slices.

Step 3 After refrigerating 24 hours, the fish should have a cooked appearance.

2. Stir in the grated lime rind, shallot, chili, and ground coriander. Mix well.

3. Cover the bowl with plastic wrap and refrigerate 24 hours, stirring occasionally during this time to ensure that the fish remains well-coated with the lime.

4. Mix the sliced peppers, green onions, and the fresh herbs together in a large bowl.

5. Put the fish mixture into a colander and drain off the juice. Add to the pepper mixture and stir in the oil, mixing well to coat evenly. Add freshly ground pepper to taste.

6. Finely shred the lettuce and arrange on a serving platter. Spread the fish mixture attractively over the lettuce and serve immediately, garnished with slices of lime, if wished.

Eggplant Bake

SERVES 6

Eggplants are wonderfully filling vegetables with very few calories – the ideal ingredient in a calorie-controlled diet.

PREPARATION: 30 mins
COOKING: 40 mins

---

2 large or 3 medium-sized eggplants
2 tsps salt
⅔ cup vinegar
2 tbsps vegetable oil
2 large onions, sliced into rings
2 green chilies, seeded and finely chopped
1-pound can chopped tomatoes
½ tsp chili powder
1 tsp crushed garlic
½ tsp ground turmeric
8 tomatoes, sliced
1¼ cups plain low-fat yogurt
1 tsp freshly ground black pepper
½ cup yellow cheese, finely grated

---

1. Cut the eggplants into ¼-inch thick slices. Arrange the slices in a shallow dish and sprinkle with 1 tsp of the salt. Pour over the vinegar, cover and marinate 30 minutes.

2. Drain the eggplants well, discarding the marinade liquid. Press the slices into a colander using the back of your hand, to remove all of the excess vinegar.

3. Heat the oil in a skillet and gently sauté the onion rings until they are golden-brown.

4. Add the chilies, the remaining salt, chopped

Step 7 Spoon half the tomato sauce over the eggplant slices in the gratin dish.

tomatoes, chili powder, garlic, and turmeric. Mix well and simmer 5-7 minutes until thick and well-blended.

5. Remove the sauce from the heat and cool slightly. Blend to a smooth purée in a liquidizer or food processor.

6. Arrange half of the eggplant slices in a lightly-greased shallow, ovenproof dish.

7. Spoon half of the tomato sauce over the eggplant, cover with the remaining eggplant, and then top with the rest of the tomato sauce, and sliced tomatoes.

8. Mix together the yogurt, black pepper, and cheese, and pour this over the tomato slices.

9. Bake in an oven preheated to 375°F, for 20-30 minutes, or until the topping bubbles and turns golden-brown. Serve hot, straight from the oven.

Chicken with 'Broiled' Peppers and Coriander

SERVES 4

'Broiling' peppers is a technique for removing the skins which also imparts a delicious flavor to this popular vegetable.

PREPARATION: 30 mins
COOKING: 1½ hrs

---

2 red peppers, halved and seeded
1 green pepper, halved and seeded
4 tbsps vegetable oil, for brushing
1 tbsp olive oil
2 tsps paprika
¼ tsp ground cumin
Pinch cayenne pepper
2 cloves garlic, crushed
2 cups canned tomatoes, drained and chopped
3 tbsps fresh chopped coriander (cilantro)
3 tbsps fresh chopped parsley
Salt, for seasoning
4 large chicken breasts, boned
1 large onion, sliced
4 tbsps flaked almonds

---

1. Put the peppers, cut side down, on a flat surface and gently press them flat. Brush the skin side with 2 tbsps of the vegetable oil and cook them under a hot broiler until the skin chars and splits.

2. Wrap the peppers in a clean kitchen towel for 10 minutes to cool, then carefully peel off the charred skin. Chop the pepper flesh into thin strips.

3. Heat the olive oil in a frying pan and gently fry all the spices and garlic for 2 minutes, stirring to prevent the garlic from browning.

4. Stir in the tomatoes, herbs, and seasoning. Simmer 15-20 minutes, or until thick. Set aside.

5. Heat the remaining vegetable oil in a flameproof casserole or Dutch oven, and sauté the chicken breasts, turning them frequently until golden on both sides.

6. Remove the chicken and set aside. Gently sauté the onion in the oil about 5 minutes, or until softened.

7. Return the chicken to the casserole with the onion and pour on about 1½ cups of water. Bring to the boil. Cover the casserole and simmer about 30 minutes, turning the chicken occasionally to prevent it from burning.

8. Remove the chicken from the casserole and boil the remaining liquid rapidly to reduce to about ⅓ cup of broth. Add the peppers and the tomato sauce, stirring well.

9. Return the chicken to the casserole, cover, and simmer very gently a further 30 minutes, or until tender.

10. Arrange the chicken on a serving platter with a little of the sauce spooned over it. Sprinkle with the flaked almonds and serve any remaining sauce separately.

Herrings with Apples

SERVES 4

The addition of apples beautifully complements the delicious and wholesome flavor of herring.

PREPARATION: 15-20 mins
COOKING: 50 mins

---

4 herrings, cleaned
2 large dessert apples
4 large potatoes, peeled and sliced
1 large onion, thinly sliced
Salt and freshly ground black pepper
⅔ cup cider
½ cup dried breadcrumbs
4 tbsps polyunsaturated margarine
1 tbsp fresh chopped parsley

---

1. Cut the heads and tails from the herrings and split them open from the underside.

2. Put the herrings, belly side down, on a flat surface, and carefully press along the back of each fish with the palm of your hand, pushing the backbone down toward the surface.

3. Turn the herrings over and with a sharp knife, carefully prise away the backbone, pulling out any loose bones as well. Do not cut the fish into separate fillets. Wash and dry them well.

4. Peel, quarter, core, and slice one of the apples. Lightly grease a shallow baking dish and layer the potatoes, apple, and onions, seasoning well with salt and pepper between layers.

Step 3
Carefully lift the backbone away from the fish with a sharp knife, pulling any loose bones out at the same time.

5. Pour the cider over the top potato layer and cover the dish with foil. Bake 40 minutes in a preheated oven at 350°F.

6. Remove the dish from the oven and arrange the fish fillets on the top. Sprinkle the breadcrumbs over them and dot with half of the margarine.

7. Increase the oven temperature to 400°F and return the dish to the oven for about 10-15 minutes, or until the fish are cooked and brown.

8. Core the remaining apple and slice into rounds, leaving the peel on. Melt the remaining margarine in a skillet and gently sauté the apple slices.

9. Remove the fish from the oven and garnish with the sautéed apple slices and chopped parsley. Serve at once.

Veal with Sorrel Stuffing

SERVES 6

Fresh sorrel has a delightful flavor, but if it is not available use spinach or silverbeet (Swiss chard).

PREPARATION: 25 mins
COOKING: 1 hr

---

2 pounds rolled leg of veal
½ cup low fat soft cheese with garlic and herbs
2 cups sorrel, finely chopped
2 tsps fresh oregano or marjoram, chopped
2 tbsps walnuts, finely chopped
Freshly ground black pepper
4 tbsps all-purpose flour
½ tsp paprika
1 egg, beaten
1 cup dried breadcrumbs
3 tbsps polyunsaturated margarine, melted

---

1. Unroll the veal roast and trim some of the fat from the outside, using a sharp knife.

2. Put the cheese, sorrel, oregano or marjoram, walnuts, and black pepper into a bowl. Mix

Step 2 Spread the filling ingredients evenly over the inside of the veal.

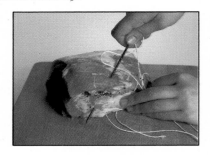

Step 2 Sew the ends of the veal together using a trussing needle and strong thread.

together, using a round-bladed knife or your hands, until the ingredients are well bound together. Spread this filling over the inside of the veal. Roll the veal up, jellyroll fashion, and stitch the ends together with a trussing needle and thick thread.

3. Dredge the veal roll with the flour and sprinkle with the paprika. Press this coating firmly over the meat, using your hands.

4. Brush the floured meat liberally with beaten egg and roll it into the dried breadcrumbs, pressing gently to make sure that all surfaces are thoroughly coated.

5. Place the coated veal in a roasting pan, brush with the melted margarine and roast in a preheated oven at 325°F, for 1 hour, or until the meat is well-cooked.

6. Allow to stand 10 minutes before slicing and serving hot, or chill and serve cold.

Tarragon Broiled Mullet

SERVES 4

Mullet is small fish that is available in the northeast. Porgy or redfish can be substituted

PREPARATION: 10 mins plus marinating
COOKING: 10-16 mins

---

4 large or 8 small red mullet, dressed, scaled,
    washed and dried
4 or 8 sprigs fresh tarragon
4 tbsps vegetable oil
2 tbsps tarragon vinegar
Salt and freshly ground black pepper

---

1. Rub the inside of each mullet with a teaspoon of salt, scrubbing hard to remove any discolored membranes inside. Rinse thoroughly.

2. Place a sprig of fresh tarragon inside each fish.

Step 1 Rub the insides of each fish with a teaspoon of salt, scrubbing briskly to remove any discolored membranes.

Step 3 Using a sharp knife, cut 2 diagonal slits on the side of each fish, taking great care not to cut right through the flesh.

3. Using a sharp knife cut 2 diagonal slits on both sides of each fish.

4. Mix together the vegetable oil, tarragon vinegar, and a little salt and pepper, in a small bowl.

5. Arrange the fish on a shallow dish and pour the tarragon vinegar marinade over it, brushing some of the mixture into the cuts on the side of the fish. Refrigerate 30 minutes.

6. Arrange the fish on a broiler pan and cook under a preheated hot broiler for 5-8 minutes per side, depending on the size of the fish. Baste frequently with the marinade while cooking. Serve with some sprigs of fresh tarragon, if liked.

Chicken with Lemon Julienne

SERVES 4-6

Lean chicken served with a tangy julienne of fresh vegetables makes a delicious entrée.

PREPARATION: 40 mins
COOKING: 55 mins

1 × 3-pound chicken
2 tbsps olive oil
2 tbsps polyunsaturated margarine
2 sticks celery
2 carrots
1 small onion, thinly sliced
1 tbsp chopped fresh basil
1 bayleaf
Juice and grated rind of 2 small lemons
⅔ cup water
Salt and freshly ground black pepper
Lemon slices, for garnish

1. Cut the chicken into 8 pieces with a sharp knife or a cook's cleaver, slicing lengthwise down the breastbone and through the backbone to halve it completely.

2. Cut the chicken in half again, slitting between the leg joint diagonally up and around the breast joint. Finally, cut the drumsticks from the leg thigh joint, and the wings from the breast joints. Remove the skin from the chicken by pulling and cutting away with a sharp knife.

3. Heat the oil and margarine in a large skillet. Gently sauté the chicken pieces, turning them frequently to brown evenly. Remove and set aside.

4. Using a sharp knife, cut the celery and carrots into pieces 1½ inches long. Cut these pieces lengthwise into long thin matchsticks.

5. Stir the carrots and celery into the chicken juices, along with the onion. Cook over a gentle heat about 3 minutes or until just beginning to soften but not brown.

6. Stir in the basil, bayleaf, lemon juice, and rind, the water, and salt and pepper. Mix well and cook 2-3 minutes. Add the chicken and bring to the boil.

7. Cover the pan and reduce the heat. Allow the casserole to simmer for about 35-45 minutes, or until the chicken is tender and the juices run clear when the meat is pierced with a sharp knife.

8. Remove the chicken and vegetables to a serving dish and discard the bayleaf.

9. Heat the sauce quickly to thicken if necessary. Spoon the sauce over the chicken and garnish with the lemon slices.

Salmon-Trout with Spinach

SERVES 6-8

PREPARATION: 35-40 mins
COOKING: 40 mins

---

1 × 2½ pound fresh whole salmon-trout, cleaned
8 cups spinach, stalks removed
1 small onion, finely chopped
4 tbsps polyunsaturated margarine
4 tbsps walnuts, roughly chopped
1 cup fresh white breadcrumbs
1 tbsp fresh chopped parsley
1 tbsp fresh chopped thyme
¼ tsp grated nutmeg
Salt and freshly ground black pepper
Juice of 2 lemons
Watercress sprigs and lemon slices, to garnish

1. Carefully slit the underside of the fish to the tip of the tail. Flatten it, belly side down, on a work surface.

2. Using the palm of your hand press down along the backbone, to push the spine downward. Turn the fish over and using a sharp knife, carefully pull the backbone away, cutting it out with scissors at the base of the head and tail.

3. Pull out any loose bones with a pair of tweezers then set the fish in the center of a large square of lightly-oiled foil.

4. Put the washed spinach into a large saucepan and sprinkle with salt. Do not add any extra water. Cover and cook over a moderate heat about 3 minutes.

5. Turn into a colander and drain well, pressing with a spoon to remove all the excess moisture. Chop very finely, using a sharp knife.

6. Fry the onion gently in 1 tbsp of the margarine until soft. Stir into the spinach along with the walnuts, breadcrumbs, herbs, nutmeg, salt, pepper, and half the lemon juice. Mix well.

7. Push the stuffing firmly into the cavity of the fish, re-shaping it as you do so. Seal the foil over the fish, but do not wrap too tightly. Place in a roasting pan and bake 35 minutes in a preheated oven at 350°F.

8. Carefully unwrap the fish and transfer to a large serving platter. Using a sharp knife, peel away the exposed skin of the fish.

9. Dot with the remaining margarine, sprinkle with the remaining lemon juice, and garnish with watercress and lemon slices.

Orange and Apricot Mousse

SERVES 4-6

This delicious light mousse makes an ideal ending to any meal.

PREPARATION: 30-50 mins plus chilling time

2 oranges
3 × 400g/14oz cans of apricots in natural juice, drained
Artificial sweetener to taste (optional)
2 tbsps unflavored gelatin
⅔ cup plain low-fat yogurt
2 egg whites
Extra orange rind, to decorate

1. Grate the rind from half of one orange using a fine grater.

2. Cut all the oranges in half and squeeze out the juice.

3. Put the drained apricots, all but 3 tbsps of the orange juice, and the orange rind into a

Step 5 Allow the fruit purée and gelatin to chill in a refrigerator until it is just beginning to set.

Step 6 Fold the egg whites carefully, but thoroughly, into the thickening fruit mixture, taking care not to overmix.

liquidizer or food processor, and purée until smooth. Pour into a large bowl and set aside.

4. Sprinkle the gelatin over the orange juice in a bowl, and allow to stand until softened.

5. Set the gelatin mixture over a pan of hot water and leave to dissolve and clear.

6. Stir the gelatin mixture into the apricot purée, along with the yogurt, mixing well to blend evenly. Refrigerate about 30 minutes until beginning to set.

7. Whisk the egg whites until they form soft peaks. Fold the whisked egg whites lightly, but thoroughly, into the partially-set apricot mixture using a metal tablespoon.

8. Divide the fruit mousse evenly into serving glasses and chill until completely set.

Apple and Golden Raisin Sorbet

SERVES 4-6

Sorbets make an ideal dessert for anyone on a low fat diet. Try this unusual combination for a real change of flavors.

PREPARATION: 10 mins, plus 4 hrs soaking and 6 hrs freezing.

3¾ cups apple juice
2 tbsps sugar
3 tbsps dried apple flakes
½ cup golden raisins
Few drops green food coloring (optional)
1 egg white

1. Put 2¼ cups of the apple juice in a heavy-based saucepan along with the sugar. Heat gently, stirring until the sugar has dissolved. Bring the apple juice to the boil and boil quickly for 5 minutes. Remove from the heat and cool completely.

2. Put the apple flakes into a bowl along with the golden raisins and the remaining apple juice. Add enough of the apple sirup to cover

Step 3 Beat the apple and golden raisin mixture with a fork until it becomes a thick purée.

Step 7 Fold the whisked egg white carefully into the slushy ice before freezing completely.

the mixture, then allow to soak 4 hours.

3. Mix the apple flake mixture together to form a pulp, adding the green coloring at this stage, if required.

4. Whisk the apple pulp into the remaining sirup, mixing thoroughly to blend evenly. Pour the apple mixture into a shallow container and freeze 2 hours or until just beginning to set.

5. Break up the partially-frozen ice using a fork or electric whisk, then return to the freezer tray and continue to freeze another hour.

6. Break up the ice crystals again, but this time mash thoroughly until they form a thick slush.

7. Whisk the egg white until it is stiff, then quickly fold in the ice slush. Return to the freezer tray and freeze until completely solid.

8. Allow the ice to soften for 15 minutes before spooning into individual sundae glasses.

Cherry Compôte

SERVES 6

Black cherries and fruit juice combine perfectly in this tasty dessert.

PREPARATION: 20 mins
COOKING: 5 mins

---

6 cups fresh black cherries
2 cups apple or grape juice
1½ tsps finely grated lemon rind
2 tbsps cornstarch or potato starch
3 tbsps brandy (optional)

---

1. Pit the cherries, using a cherry pitter or the rounded end of a potato peeler.

2. Put the pitted cherries into a saucepan, along with the apple or grape juice and the lemon rind. Bring to the boil over a moderate

Step 1 Pit the cherries using a cherry pitter or the rounded end of a potato peeler.

Step 4 Blend the cornstarch or potato starch with 5 tbsps of the cherry juice.

heat, then simmer 10 minutes, or until the cherries are gently poached.

3. Remove the cherries from the juice with a slotted spoon, leaving the juice in the saucepan. Arrange the cherries in a serving bowl.

4. Blend the cornstarch or potato starch with 5 tbsps of the cherry juice.

5. Add the blended cornstarch or potato starch to the cherry juice in the pan, and bring to the boil, stirring constantly until the sauce has thickened. Stir in the brandy if using.

6. Pour the thickened cherry sauce over the cherries in the bowl, and chill well before serving.

Spiced Oranges with Honey and Mint

SERVES 4

An unusual combination of flavors blend to create this light and very refreshing dessert.

PREPARATION: 20 mins
COOKING: 5 mins

1¼ cups clear honey
2 cups water
2 large sprigs of fresh mint
12 whole cloves
4 large oranges
4 small sprigs of mint, to garnish

---

1. Put the honey and the water into a heavy-based saucepan. Add the mint and cloves, and slowly bring to the boil.

2. Stir the mixture to dissolve the honey and boil rapidly 5 minutes, or until the liquid is very sirupy.

3. Cool the mixture completely, then strain the syrup through a nylon sieve into a jug or bowl to remove the sprigs of mint and cloves.

Step 3 Strain the cool sirup through a nylon sieve into a jug or bowl to remove the sprigs of mint and cloves.

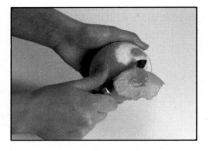

Step 4 Carefully pare the rind from one of the oranges using a potato peeler.

4. Using a potato peeler, carefully pare the rind very thinly from one orange, making sure that no white part comes away with the rind. Cut the pared orange rind into very fine shreds with a sharp knife.

5. Put the shreds of orange peel into a small bowl and cover with boiling water. Allow to stand until cold then drain completely, reserving only the strips of peel. Stir the strips of peel into the honey sirup and chill well.

6. Peel the oranges completely, removing all the skin and especially the white parts.

7. Slice the oranges into thin rounds using a sharp knife. Arrange the orange rounds onto four individual serving plates.

8. Pour the chilled sirup over the oranges on the plates and garnish with the small sprigs of mint just before serving.

Index

Tomato and Pepper Ice, a refreshing appetizer.